NATIONAL GEOGRAPHIC

Feelings

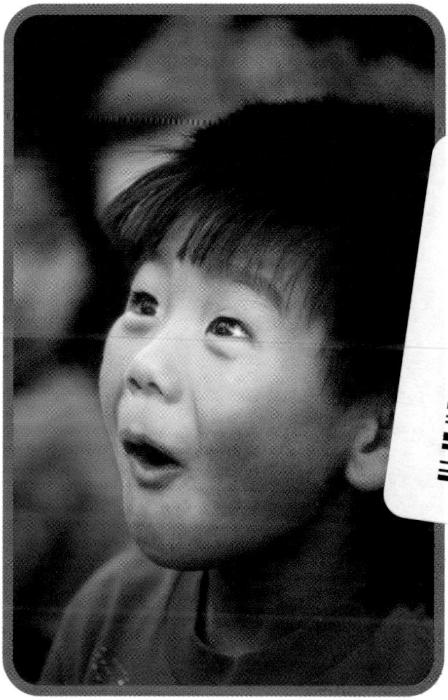

Jan Pritchett

How do I feel?

How do I feel?

21

How do I feel?

How do I feel?

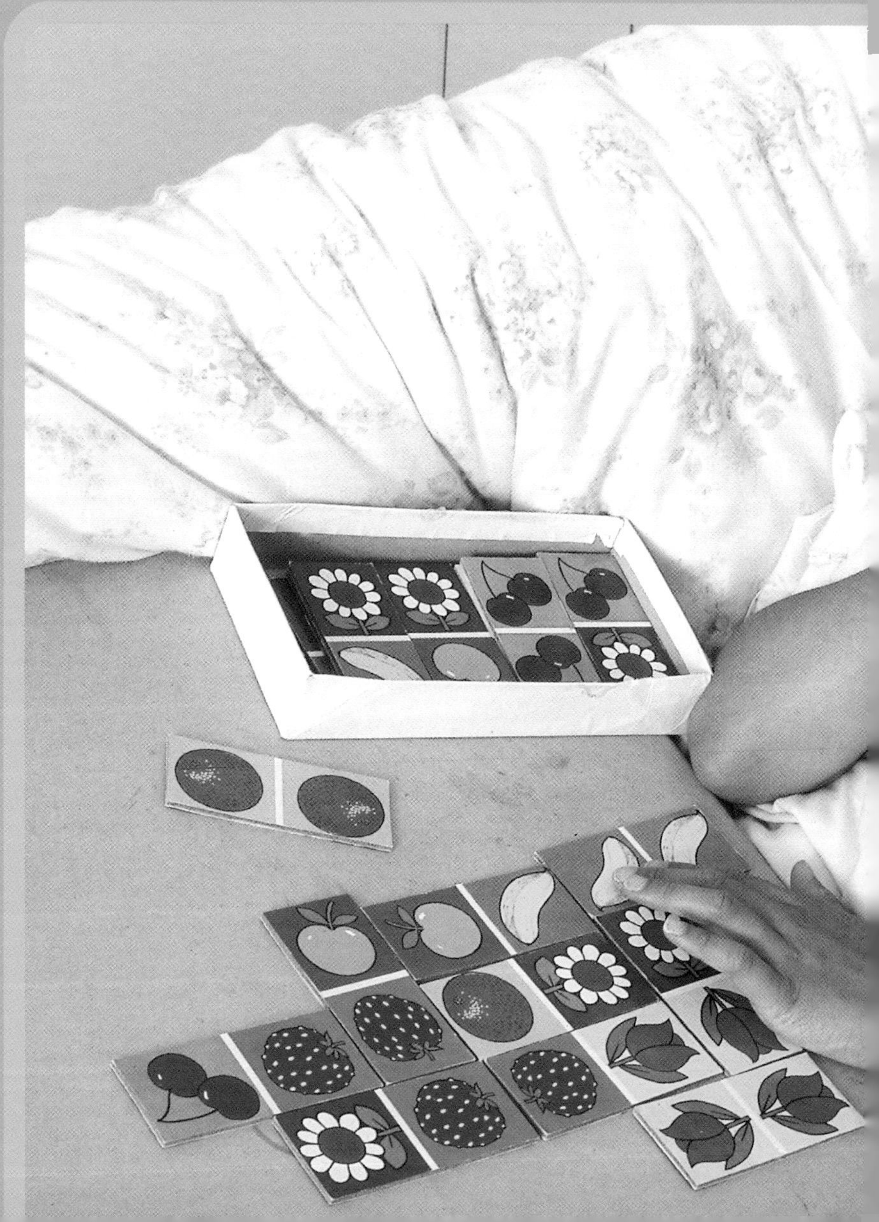

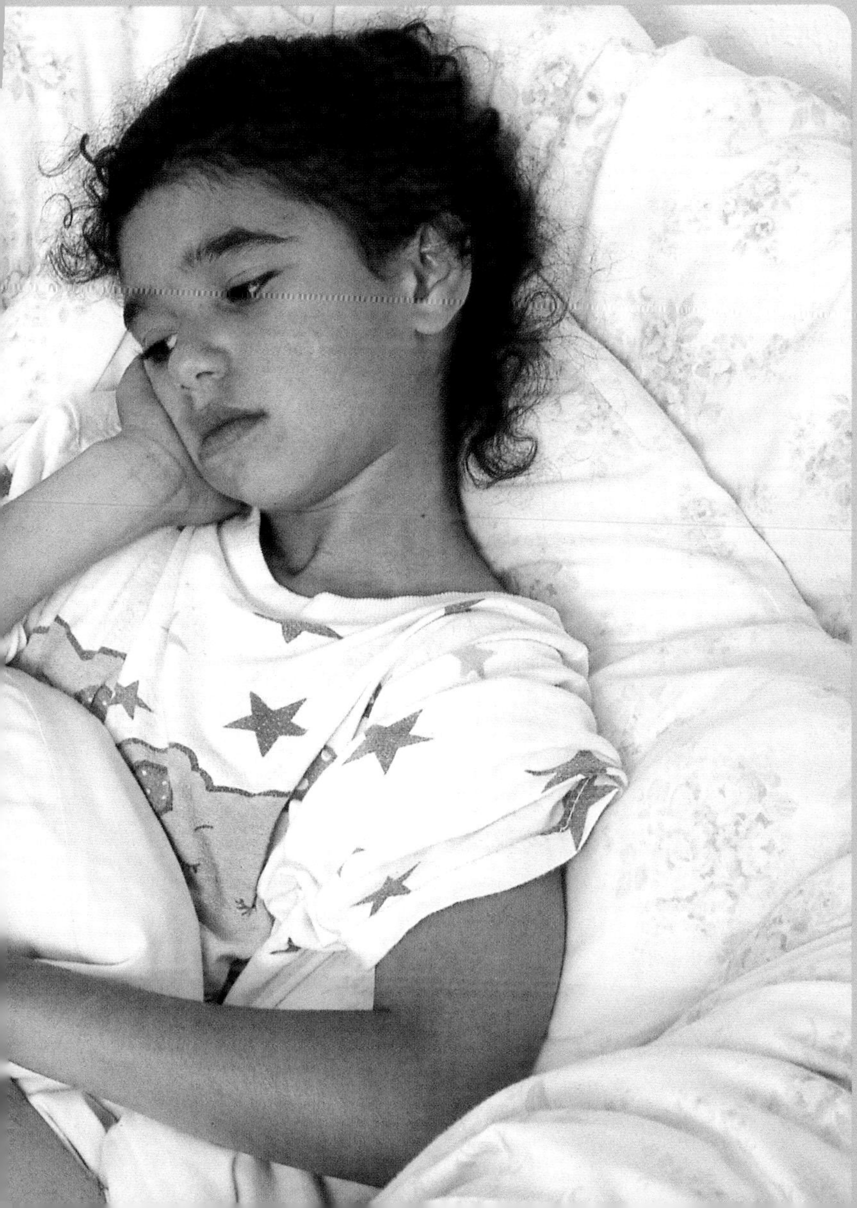

How do I feel?

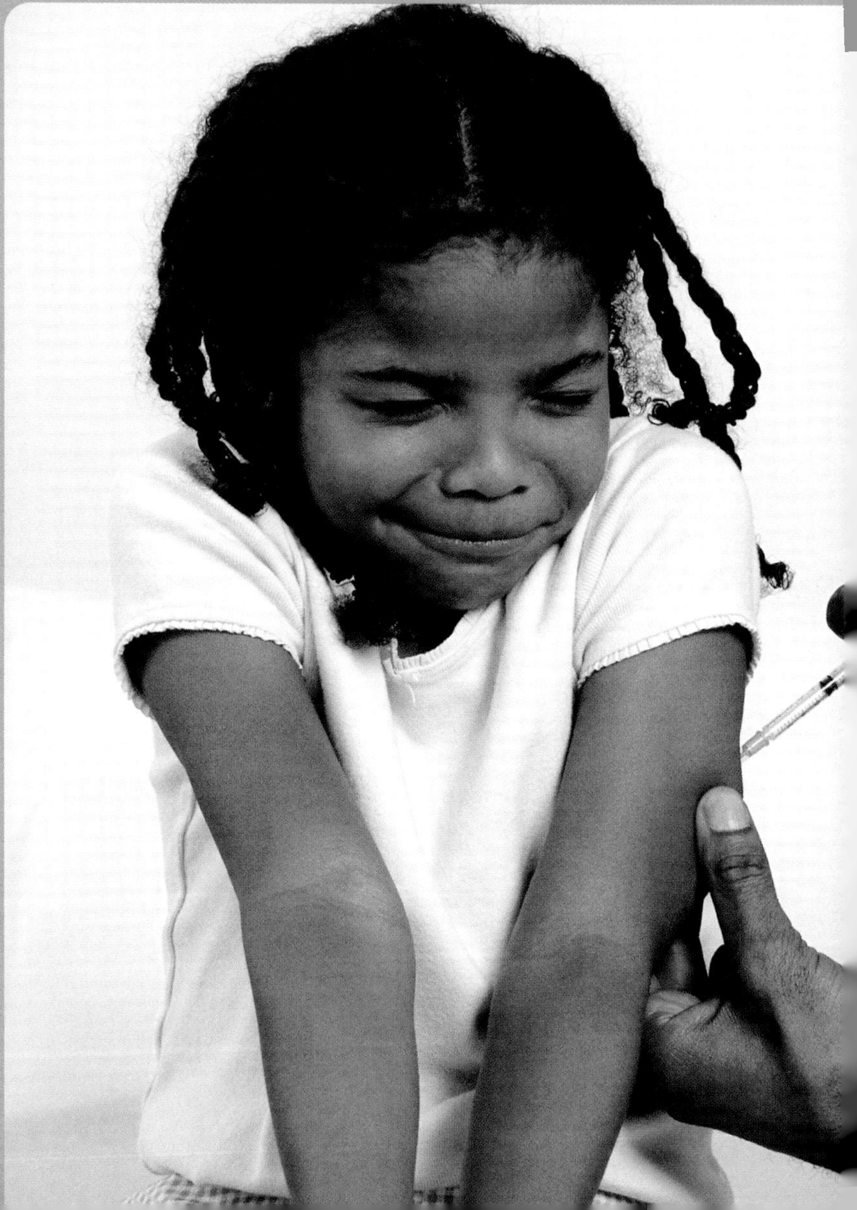

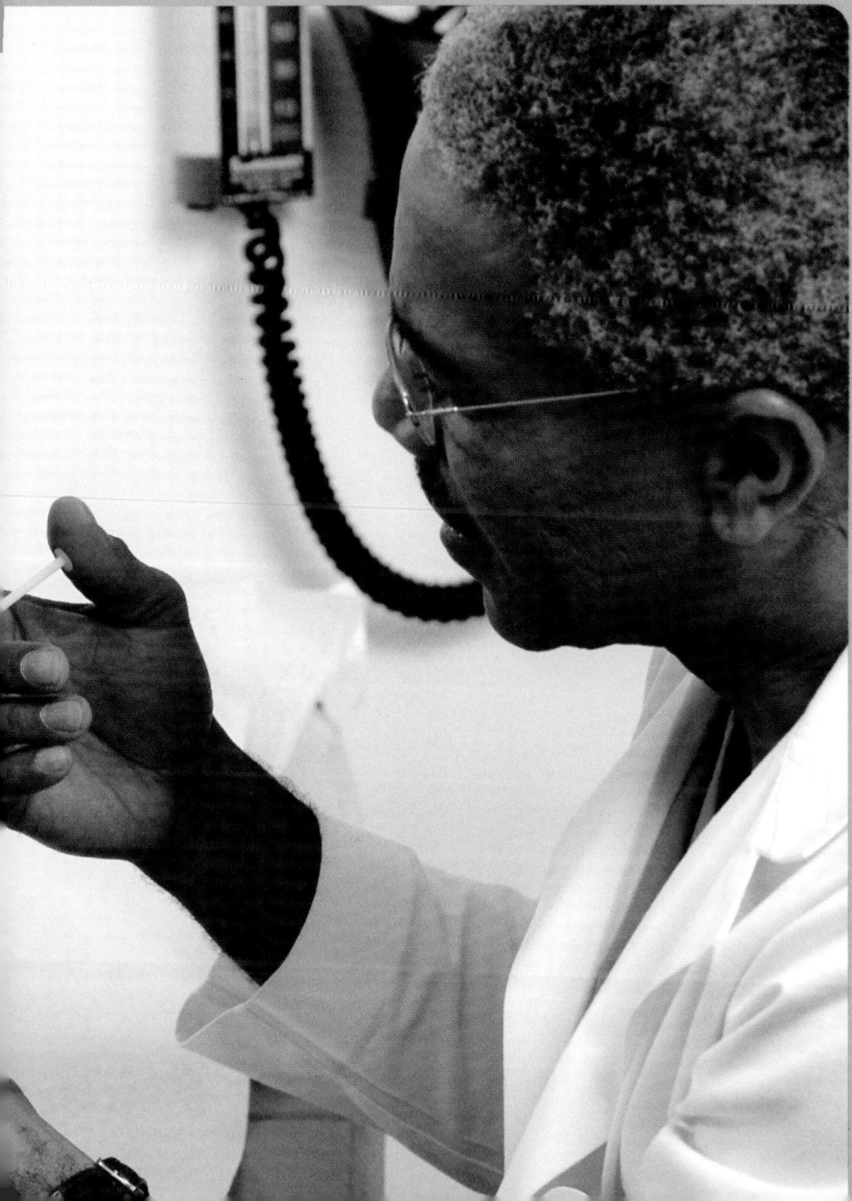

How do I feel?